D0048808

Hermit Crab Care

Habitat, Food, Health, Behavior, Shells, and lots more. The complete Hermit Crab Pet Book...

Charles Sure

Foreword

Many of us feel a powerful need to share our lives with pets, both for the fascination of living with an interesting, intelligent, engaging animal and because our pets give us relaxation, companionship, and unconditional affection.

I have had many animal friends in my life. As a young person with indulgent parents, I had the space to keep a lovely menagerie of dogs and cats that were my constant companions.

We had a large and beautiful aquarium, there were a few birds here and there, and when I was in college I kept hamsters and a guinea pig. (That was rather against the dorm rules, by the way, but we pulled it off.)

My love for animals is so great that I've put seeds out for the birds and peanuts for the squirrels only to buy more for the raccoons and opossums that decided to help themselves.

My friends and family tolerated what they laughingly called the "All You Can Eat Critter Bar" I ran on my patio for many years. There were stray cats in the mix as well, and as much as I hate to admit it, a rather large rat with a crippled paw who was extremely well behaved and never brought any of his friends around to infest the yard.

My initial association with hermit crabs, however, was the result of someone basically taking advantage of my good graces. A friend at work asked if I might look after his son's "leftover" hermit crabs while the family went on vacation over the summer.

The son dumped the "hermies" on his parents when he went off to college and then they dumped the crabs on me. By the time my friend and his wife came home, it was clear they didn't want the crabs back. I had already improved the crabitat, added furniture, purchased a new under tank heater, and joined a hermit crab discussion forum.

It seems to have worked out for all concerned. All but one of the hermies is still alive five years later, and I have found life with the crabs to be amazingly convivial.

I did have to invest in a much better lid as my cats were a little too fascinated at first, but the crabitat is now safely out of reach and everyone gets along just fine.

My grandmother used to say that good fences make good neighbors. Good segregation, high shelves, and tight aquarium lids make for a successful multi-species household.

This book is my attempt to put together information for people new to crab keeping. My experience is actually not all that unusual. While you might not think of hermit crabs as rescue animals, they get abandoned fairly often.

Why? Because people buy them thinking they won't live long, and ten years later the crabs are still there. Yes, that's right. Surprised are you? Hermit crabs can live a decade or more! Which is actually delightful when you think about it.

Many of the smaller animals that can be housed in tanks, and that are so convenient for people living in apartments die all too quickly. It really doesn't matter what kind of pet you have. If you've invested time and attention on its care, you will be affected when it dies.

Hermit crabs can be with you quite a while. They have excellent personalities. They're curious and intelligent. They like to interact with their humans. They're clean, have no odor, and are incredibly low maintenance. In short? Hermit crabs are fun.

Exclusive Free Offer

Join other Hermit Crab lovers and owners in our unique **FREE** club – Exclusive to owners of this book.

See page 28 on how to join easily in seconds (and free). Receive discounts on hermit crab supplies like food and housing. Connect with other members to share knowledge and experience, or ask questions. The best place for lovers of these amazing creatures.

Table of Contents

Foreword 1

Exclusive Free Offer.. 4

Table of Contents 5

Chapter 1 – The Hermit Crab's World................................ 11

Land vs. Aquatic Hermit Crabs 11

What Are Land Hermit Crabs? 12

True Crabs vs. Hermit Crabs? 12

Why Hermit Crabs Aren't Hermits 13

Don't Adopt Wild Hermit Crabs 15

Hermies Kept as Pets 15

    Purple Pinchers.. 16

    Ecuadorian 17

    Other Varieties... 18

Hermit Crab Anatomy.. 19

    The Exoskeleton and Molting.................................... 19

    Borrowing a Protective Shell 19

    Legs and Claws... 20

    Gills and Mouth Parts.. 21

    Eyes, Eyestalks, and Antennae................................. 21

Table of Contents

Lifespan 22

Hermit Crabs and Children 22

Crabs and Other Pets 24

One Crab or More? 24

Pros and Cons of Hermit Crabs 24

Exclusive FREE Offer – How to Join 28

Chapter 2 – Buying Your Hermit Crabs 29

Where to Make Your Purchase 29

What to Consider Before Buying 31

Gender Doesn't Matter 31

Size Does Matter 31

How to Pick Hermit Crabs 32

Signs of Good Health 32

Handle the Crabs 33

Introduce the Group 33

The All Important Extra Shells 34

Will It Fit? 34

Beware of Buyer's Remorse 34

Recognizing a Good Fit 35

Picking Shells 35

Table of Contents

Collecting Beach Shells... 36

Buying Shells Online 37

Bringing Your Hermies Home 38

New Hermie on the Block... 39

Chapter 3 - Hermit Crab Care 41

Designing Your Crabitat 42

The Isolation Tank.. 43

Positioning the Crabitat... 43

Temperature Control 44

Humidity Control 45

Natural Sea Sponge.. 46

Lighting 47

Bedding or Substrate 47

Substrates to Avoid... 48

Collecting Beach Sand 49

Adding Shelters... 50

Food and Water Dishes 50

Saltwater for Your Hermies.. 51

Decorating the Crabitat 52

Your Hermie Shopping List.. 53

Table of Contents

Consider Stressors and Toxins 55

Don't Use Painted Shells 56

Pay Attention to Air Quality 56

Misting and Bathing 57

How to Bathe Your Crabs 57

Misting Your Hermies 58

Handling and Bonding 59

Picking Up Your Hermies 59

Playing with Hermie 60

Chapter 4 - Feeding and Crabitat Maintenance 61

Commercial Hermit Crab Foods 61

Fresh Foods 62

Special Treats 64

Foods to Avoid 64

Sources of Calcium 65

Sources of Carotene 66

Feeding Times 66

Use Handfeeding 68

Hydration is Crucial 68

Crabitat Maintenance 69

Table of Contents

Chapter 5 - Health, Behavior, and Breeding 72

Signs of a Healthy Hermit Crab 72

Preventive "Medicine" 73

Understanding Molting.. 74

Unexpected Molting 75

During and After the Molt............................ 76

Molting Tragedies 77

Understanding Normal Behavior 77

Crabs Make Noise 78

Wrecking the Crabitat 78

Wrestling and Game Play 79

Aggression and Fighting................................ 79

Hermie Seems Withdrawn................................... 80

Dealing with Insects in the Crabitat 81

Combating Pests.................................... 82

Clean and Disinfect the Crabitat..................... 83

What Attracted the Pests? 84

Breeding Hermies?................................ 85

Chapter 6 - Frequently Asked Questions 86

Afterword.. 102

Table of Contents

Relevant Websites 105

Glossary 109

Index... 112

Chapter 1 – The Hermit Crab's World

If you want a very scary answer to "What is a hermit crab?" you can look these whimsical little creatures up in an encyclopedia. You will be rather archly informed that they are "decapod crustaceans of the superfamily Paguroidea." Unless you're in a marine biology class, that's not very helpful, is it?

Land vs. Aquatic Hermit Crabs

To clarify from the beginning there are two broad categories of hermit crabs: land and aquatic. As the name implies, land crabs live on the land and aquatic crabs live completely under the water.

You will certainly see aquatic hermit crabs in saltwater marine aquaria, but all of the hermit crabs that are sold exclusively as pets — and the hermit crabs that will be covered in this book — are land crabs and will be referred to simply as "hermit crabs" or "hermies."

What Are Land Hermit Crabs?

Land hermit crabs, like their underwater cousins, are related to shrimp and lobsters. They are popular pets kept by enthusiasts in glass aquaria called "crabitats" and are readily available in most pet stores.

Hermit crabs are not, however "typical" companion animals. You're not going to take your crab for a walk, but by the same token, he isn't going to need a litter box. Hermit crabs take up very little space and provide you with a great deal of entertainment, but all too often they are "impulse buy" pets, which is NEVER a good idea!

It doesn't matter how physically small they are or how low maintenance they may be, hermit crabs are still living creatures with specific needs that must be met. For that reason, it's imperative that you understand these unique animals in order to care for them correctly.

True Crabs vs. Hermit Crabs?

"True" crabs are close relatives of both shrimp and lobsters. They have five pairs of legs. They use four of those pairs for walking and the front pair, which we think of as their pinchers or "claws," for feeding and self-defense.
All of these creatures have very short abdomens that are encased in a hard protective shell. If you've ever ordered

lobster in a fancy restaurant, you'll know just how hard that shell really is!

Hermit crabs are like true crabs in that they live on the shore near the ocean and have five pairs of legs, but the key difference is that they have no all-inclusive shell of their own.

Hermies borrow snail shells to protect their soft bodies. The reason they pick the snail shells is that the internal structure curves perfectly to match the crab's anatomy.

Why Hermit Crabs Aren't Hermits

Hermit crabs are one of those creatures that suffer from a really bad name, not for anything they've ever done, but for what humans decided to call them!

Hermit crabs are NOT hermits. They have no desire to go off and live by themselves. They are very social creatures and in the wild are often found in groups of 100 or more.

They do, however, carry everything they "own" on their backs, and they do retreat into their shells when they're frightened.

Hermies are also nocturnal. During the day, they hide under rocks and leaves, crawl into crevices in trees or driftwood, or burrow into the sand. These behaviors hide them from predators and protect them from harsh sunlight. But those are the only things they do that qualify them as actual "hermits."

As the sun begins to set and the temperature drops, hermit crabs come out to wander the beach looking for food. They live by scavenging and will basically eat whatever is available whether it's meat or fruit. Hermies will even consume bark from decaying driftwood.

A great deal of a hermit crab's time is spent shopping for real estate. They're always on the lookout for a better shell than the one they currently occupy.

By nature, hermies are adventuresome. Their nocturnal wanderings often take them a mile or more from the shoreline.

The fastest way to have an unhappy, unhealthy hermit crab is to ask him to be a hermit! "Hermies" do not like to live alone and they absolutely have to have intellectual stimulation.

From the beginning, if you plan to keep hermit crabs as pets, the best philosophy you can adopt is, "The more the merrier." You'll need to put care and thought into their crabitat, and redecorate often to stay ahead of their native curiosity and intelligence.

Don't Adopt Wild Hermit Crabs

It's not a good idea to find a hermit crab in the wild and take it home as a pet. The chances of picking up a female on her way back to the sea to lay her eggs is too high.

Beyond this obvious disruption of the natural cycle of life, hermies adopted in this way almost always die. The stress of the transition, and the difference in environmental quality from the wild to a crabitat is too great.

Also, in many areas, it's illegal to collect wild hermit crabs. No one really wants to have an encounter with a game warden or a park ranger, or pay a big fine over a tiny hermit crab! Just go to the pet store!

Hermies Kept as Pets

As much as I'd like to give you a rundown of all the types of hermit crabs in the world, there are 1100 species and this book isn't intended as an encyclopedia!
Fortunately, there are only half a dozen hermies typically kept as pets, and within that group only two that you will

find readily available in pet stores: the Purple Pincher and the Ecuadorian.

Purple Pinchers

The Purple Pincher hermit crab, also called the Caribbean hermit crab, soldier crab, the West Atlantic crab, or the tree crab is the one you'll see most often living as a companion animal.

They're actually very pretty little creatures, with multiple colors on their legs across a range of shades including red, orange, yellow, purple, and tan.

The front pinchers or "claws" — especially the left, which is typically larger — is almost always purple, hence the name. They have long, slender eyestalks and dot-shaped eyes.

The Purple Pincher is a little less active than the other commonly kept species, the Ecuadorian hermit crab, but they are more willing to use their pinchers if they're scared.

The scientific name for the species is *Coenobita clypeatus*. They are indigenous to the greater Caribbean, but are also found in the Florida Keys, the Virgin Islands, the West Indies, and Venezuela.

Individual Purple Pinchers are generally sold for around $9-$10 / £5.51-£6.13 each.

Ecuadorian Hermit

Ecuadorian hermit crabs are one of the smallest species of hermies at an average size of just 0.47 inches or 12 millimeters.

Their scientific name is *Coenobita compressus*. In most cases this species exhibits a tan body, but they can be bright yellow, orange, or dark gray. Occasionally, individuals will have a blue to green tint on their bodies or inside the legs.

The eyestalks of the Ecuadorian are similar to that of the Purple Pincher, but its eyes are shaped like commas. They have a particular preference for shells with round, wide openings.

They are fast, active, and excellent runners, rapidly switching gears to move forward, backwards, and sideways without ever slowing down.

They are also the species that is most active during the daylight hours, which is one of the principle reasons they are attractive in the pet trade. Do not even think about keeping an Ecuadorian Hermit without giving him lots of things to climb on.

As a result, you have to be careful about escapes with this species as there have been reports of them climbing the sealant in the corners of glass aquariums.

Typically, individuals are priced at around \$7-\$8 / £4.28-£4.90 each.

Other Varieties

There are four other types of hermit crabs that do show up in the pet trade. Not all are commonly available, but you will see:

- Indonesian Purple Hermit Crab (*Coenobita brevimanus*), the largest of the hermit crabs, and the one considered to be the most mellow and relaxed.

- Cavipes (*Coenobita cavipes*), a shy crab prized for its appearance. A cavipes' body is black, blue or red, and its antennae are also red.

- Rugs or Ruggies (*Coenobita rugosus*) is also called the "crying" hermit crab for the unusual sounds it makes when it's upset. It comes in all shades including bright red, peach, chocolate, blue, brown, and white.

- Red or Strawberry Hermit Crab (*Coenobita prelates*) is a rare, bright orange-red crab with distinct white bumps on its legs and claws.

You will have a great deal of difficulty finding any of these hermit crabs in pet stores, although they are becoming more readily available from expert breeders.

All six of these popular species require the same type of care, however, so there's no need to learn specific husbandry standards for each one.

Hermit Crab Anatomy

The easiest way to understand the anatomy of your hermit crabs is to think of the three main parts of their bodies:

- head
- thorax
- abdomen

Only a portion of their bodies have an effective protective covering, however.

The Exoskeleton and Molting

The crab's entire body is covered with an exoskeleton made of chitin, but it is only over the head and back that this material forms a hard carapace.

The only way a hermit crab can grow is to "molt" or shed its old exoskeleton for a newer, larger version. This is the same process experienced by many insect species.

Borrowing a Protective Shell

The hermie's abdomen, however, is very soft and can be easily injured, which is why hermit crabs move into abandoned snail shells for protection.

As I mentioned earlier, the spiral of a snail's shell curves to the right, perfectly matching the curvature of the hermit crab's body.

Hermies use their fourth and fifth sets of legs to hold themselves inside their shells. The fifth pair of legs are extremely flexible and equipped with tiny pinchers, which the crab uses to push feces from the interior of the shell and to groom their abdomens.

Legs and Claws

In total, hermit crabs have five pairs of legs, but only three sets are typically visible. The first pair of legs are called chelipeds and are the hermit's claws.

The left claw is always larger than the right and is very useful to the crab when it's climbing. The left claw is also used as a means of self-defense and in threat displays.

If the hermit retreats entirely inside its shell, the left claw is used to seal the entrance. The smaller right claw is used as a secondary aid to climbing and when eating. The second and third pairs of legs are ambulatory or walking legs.

Gills and Mouth Parts

There are three paired appendages about the mouth, the maxillipeds, which the crab uses to hold food for nibbling. These same appendages help in cleaning and grooming.

Hermies have gills, but they don't have to be submerged in water to breathe. In fact, if they can't escape from the water, they will drown.

Their small gills are located just above the legs on the sides of the thorax and must be kept moist at all times.

Eyes, Eyestalks, and Antennae

The hermit crab's eyes are located on stalks, which are distinct from its longer paired antennae found below the eyestalks.

Think of the antennae as roughly analogous to a cat's whiskers. Crabs use them to feel around and even to touch items with which they come into contact.

There are shorter antennules between the crab's eyes that are sensitive to odors. These structures aid the crab in locating food.

As if these complimentary sensory systems were not enough, however, the second pair of legs are also sensitive and gather information from the crab's environment after the fashion of a third set of antennae.

This ability is attributable to the presence of setae, which bristle out from the legs and act as receptors for touch. These structures are also specialized by function, with longer setae designed to detect hard surfaces, and shorter ones to feel movements in water.

Lifespan

I want to very quickly dispel the notion that hermit crabs are short-term pets. If cared for properly, hermies can easily live a decade. Don't make the mistake of thinking you are getting hermit crabs for children as "short-term pets." You'll only wind up caring for the crabs when your son or daughter goes off to college.

Hermit Crabs and Children

With the proper amount of adult supervision, children can do most of the work to care for hermit crabs on their own, but it's a good idea to make a checklist of daily chores. As the parent, you need to ensure that these tasks are actually performed, especially where humidity and temperature levels are concerned.

Also, make sure that your child washes his or her hands before and after handling the crabs. Since younger children are not consistent in their hygiene habits, this is a protection for all concerned.

Children must understand that hermit crabs are living creatures, not toys. If a hermit crab is dropped from even a short height onto a hard floor, the impact can be fatal.

Hermies are susceptible to many kinds of stress. They need to rest during the day, and they don't like to be poked and jostled around all the time. They won't do well in high levels of noise or with a lot of harassment.

All children must be taught to treat animals of any species gently and with kindness. Hermit crabs certainly cannot harm anyone or anything, but they can suffer great injury to themselves, and will die quickly if they do not receive appropriate care.

Crabs and Other Pets

It is generally a mistake to assume that other pets in the home will completely ignore the presence of a tank of hermit crabs. Dogs may represent a lesser danger, but a cat will certainly be intrigued by the crabs and will try to get into the crabitat.

If you bring hermit crabs into a home with existing pets, make sure that you have a secure lid on the crabitat that cannot be pried off. Keep the tank up high, and eliminate avenues of access.

One Crab or More?

MORE. Never try to keep just one hermit crab. These creatures are very social and are much, much happier living in groups. Crabs that are housed alone become highly stressed and will eventually fall ill and die. Two crabs are good, but three or more are better.

Pros and Cons of Hermit Crabs

Frankly, it's never easy to put together a list of pros and cons for any pet. Some people think taking a dog for a walk every day sounds like absolute heaven, while others cringe at the idea and prefer a nice indoor cat with a litter box.

Hermit crabs are, by definition, exotic pets. For that reason alone, you need to be absolutely sure you're doing the right thing before you bring hermies home. And do note that I used the plural. Hermit crabs need company. You will need to keep more than one.

With these ideas in mind, interpret each of the following points for yourself and decide if they are positives or negatives in regard to keeping hermit crabs as companion animals.

- Hermit crabs are quiet.

I do have to add a disclaimer here. While hermit crabs won't bark and keep the neighbors awake, they are very busy at night and love to rearrange things in their crabitat.

If you put them in the bedroom, you may be surprised at just how much noise they can make at night.

- Hermit crabs don't take up a lot of space.

It is true that in relation to other, larger animals, hermit crabs have minimal space requirements. You will, however, need to have the right location for the crabitat. It must be out of direct sunlight and in a spot where you can maintain the correct temperature and humidity.

- Hermit crabs don't trigger allergies.

The hypoallergenic aspect of keeping hermit crabs as pets really is not subject to much interpretation. If you sneeze and have an adverse reaction to small mammals including dogs, cats, and rabbits, you won't face the same struggle with a tank full of hermit crabs.

- Hermit crabs are clean, and do not smell.

Again, the cleanliness aspect of hermit crab care is a hard point to see in any but a positive light. They are not difficult to care for, and with minimal maintenance, they will be quite happy in their crabitat for years.

- Hermit crabs are inexpensive.

As compared to a pedigree dog or cat, hermit crabs are downright cheap. You will, however, have a number of things to buy in the beginning, but after those first set-up costs, you won't be taking your crabs to the veterinarian, getting them shots, or having to pay for a license tag.

- Hermit crabs don't outgrow their habitats.

I can truthfully say that hermit crabs are some of the most contented pets you could ask for. They do perfectly well in a glass aquarium for years, and they don't outgrow their initial space.

Exclusive FREE Offer – How to Join

Join other Hermit Crab lovers in our unique **FREE** club –
Exclusive to owners of this book.

It's quick and easy to sign up. You can receive discounts on
hermit crab food, supplies and more including connecting
with other owners. Here's how in 2 simple steps…

Step 1

Go to http://www.HermitCrabBook.com
Enter your name and email address and click 'Join.'

Step 2

Confirm your subscription. As soon as you sign up we'll
send you an email asking you to confirm the details are
correct. Just click the link in the email and you'll be joined
free.

If you don't receive the email please check your spam
folder and that you used the correct email address.

It's as easy as that. Any questions please email me
charles@bleppublishing.com and where possible I'll help.

Chapter 2 – Buying Your Hermit Crabs

Unlike many exotic pets, hermit crabs aren't difficult to find. You can buy your hermit crabs and have them home pretty much within the hour if you live in a large town.

If you are buying your hermit crabs at a pet store, make sure you have done all research prior to shopping. You will be better prepared if you do your homework ahead of time.

Where to Make Your Purchase

Chance are very good that in order to purchase your hermit crab you'll simply head down to your local big box pet store. Generally, you will get a 24-hour health guarantee with the promise of a refund if the crab dies.

The employees at the store will be very good in helping you to find all the things you need to care for your new crab — and probably several things you don't need — but they are rarely if ever experts or even knowledgeable about hermit crabs.

If you can find a smaller, local "Mom and Pop" store, you may luck into someone who actually does understand basic hermit crab care and can perhaps even distinguish one species from another.

In general, however, smaller stores will only have Purple Pinchers because they are so easy to acquire.

What to Consider Before Buying

For most people, buying hermit crabs amounts to walking into the store and saying, "I'll take three." There are, however, some things you do need to take into consideration, or ignore completely, starting with gender.

Gender Doesn't Matter

There really is no concern over the gender of the crabs you select. Males and females exhibit no differences in personality, and without access to the ocean, breeding cannot occur.

Beyond these facts, it's almost impossible to tell the genders apart. The only real way to make the distinction is to look at the back walking legs, and that has to be done with the crab outside the shell.

If you try to force a hermit to come out of its shell, you could possibly kill the creature. All in all, gender is a non-issue.

Size Does Matter

It's best to pick crabs of different sizes. Crabs of the same size will be more prone to fight over new shells. It's quite natural for hermies to trade houses within a community, so having a mix of sizes will help to maximize the use of the extra shells you provide for your pets.

How to Pick Hermit Crabs

First, take a good look around the store itself. You can tell a great deal about the probable condition of the animals from the state of the facility. If the tanks in the fish section are dirty, or the small animal cages are filthy, it's clear that no basic maintenance is being done.

Hermit crabs need tanks that are humid (more than 70%) and warm. They should not be kept anywhere with a draft, or in direct sunlight. Both are almost a guarantee that the crabs you buy will be stressed and potentially sick.

Even in the store, the crabitat should have lots of intellectual stimulation for the crabs, with hiding boxes and plenty of things to climb. The food and water dishes should be clean, and it should be clear that the bedding is changed regularly.

Hermits should never be housed with other species like frogs, turtles, or lizards, and they should not be kept in a tank with any standing water.

Even if the crabs are kept by themselves, overcrowding is often an issue in pet shop settings. Make sure all the crabs have room to move and places to hide.

Signs of Good Health

Hermit crabs that are healthy and in good shape are:

- active and curious

- completely intact, with no missing appendages
- living in a clean shell that is the correct size

If you find a tank of listless crabs with obvious physical damage, and if the water has an odor and shows signs of mold or insect activity, do not buy from the population.

Also, don't buy a crab that is molting. The creature will be in a highly vulnerable state and can suffer fatal stress if moved. As a hallmark of sound husbandry, molting crabs should never be kept in a tank with non-molting crabs.

Handle the Crabs

It's a good idea to handle your prospective pets. Gently pick up the crab by the back of the shell and place it in the palm of your hand. Even if the crab is in its shell when you pick it up, the response of a healthy crab to being handled will be to emerge and find out what's going on.

If the crab comes out and tries to use its big claw to dig into your hand, pass on the purchase. This is a sign of stress and aggression. Hermit crabs are friendly and even affectionate by nature, and certainly docile.

Introduce the Group

When you've picked out three crabs you like, place them in proximity to one another and make sure they all get along. If there are any signs of aggression, remove that crab and pick another.

The All Important Extra Shells

You need to keep plenty of extra shells for your hermies to move into. A hermit crab is always looking for the next "best shell in the world."

Will It Fit?

Hermit crabs have a perfect system for judging if a new shell will work for them. The crab inserts his left claw into the shell's opening and down into the canal. If the claw fits with what he judges to be enough extra room, he progresses to step two.

The crab begins to roll the shell around to remove debris and to ensure that no one else is camped out inside. When he's ready, he positions himself so that his abdomen will be minimally exposed during the transition, and proceeds to move into the new shell.

Beware of Buyer's Remorse

The crab doesn't, however, turn loose of his old address until he's certain the new shell is perfect. He does this by holding on to the former shell with one walking leg.

It's not at all unusual for the crab to spend a few minutes in the new shell, decide he doesn't like it, and go right back to the original.

This is the sort of behavior that makes hermits so much fun to watch. They're very particular in their habits, and highly individualistic in their personalities.

Recognizing a Good Fit

It won't take long for you to develop a practiced eye to get new shell choices for your crabs. A shell that is a good fit is one that will allow the crab to retreat completely inside and use his large claw as a "door" to block the entrance.

For every crab that you bring home, get at least two or three shells that are larger sizes than the one the crab is currently occupying.

Do not scrimp on extra shells! Hermits take this matter of real estate so seriously, they can get it in their determined little brains to kick someone else out of their home.

One crab will approach another from behind and begin to rock his shell back and forth trying to get the current resident to turn loose and abandon his home.
A territorial battle will then ensue, and it's not unusual for the participants to lose limbs — or life — in the resulting melee.

Picking Shells

There is no rhyme or reason to the matter of shell swapping with hermit crabs. Individual crabs do, however, show clear preferences for a particular type of shell while others seem to be born shoppers.

Sometimes they switch shells because the one they have doesn't fit well, or because there's some damage to the shell. At other times, there seems to be no motivation for moving to a new home than simple boredom.

Shell fights can and do occur when two crabs go after the same vacant shell, or one decides he wants a currently occupied shell. The aggression can be serious enough for physical harm to result.

Always make sure that a crab that has just gone through a molt has a slightly larger shell available.

Don't buy heavy shells. Remember, the crab has to lug that thing around! In general, hermies prefer shells with circular "front doors" that are lined with mother-of-pearl, which feels smoother on their bodies.

Ecuadorian crabs, however, like shells with oval openings that are wider and flatter.

Never give a crab a new shell that is broken, chipped, or damaged in any way or that is showing evidence of mold growth. Always check for any of these possible defects during your pet's bath time.

Collecting Beach Shells

Once you develop an eye for picking shells that will fit your hermies, it's perfectly alright to collect shells from the shoreline if you live close to the ocean.

Do not, however, give the shells to your pets immediately. Boil any shells you collect for at least five minutes in dechlorinated water. This will remove all dirt and accumulated residue as well as kill any parasites that might be along for the ride.

Allow the shells to cool thoroughly before putting them in the crabitat.

You can buy more exotic shells online, but make sure that you are buying from a reputable dealer. There is a black market trade in illegal sea shells.

Buying Shells Online

Sites like The Hermit Crab Patch at HermitCrabPatch.com sell beautiful collections of shells and provide sizing materials to help their customers make their selections.

They also offer packs of 10 shells in varying sizes for $12-$20 / £7.35-£12.25. Individual shells may sell for as low as $0.50 / £0.31 to around $5 /£3.06.

Bringing Your Hermies Home

On the way home from the pet store, your hermies will probably be housed in a cardboard box. Make sure they are not thrown around inside the container. If possible, line it with a towel to give them additional cushioning.

This is actually a good opportunity to go ahead and purchase a small plastic crate that you can later use as an isolation tank for molting. Bear in mind, however, that a plastic container will only work as a secondary tank if you can maintain the internal temperature and humidity. More on this topic in the next chapter.

A "critter keeper" is ideal for travel purposes. These plastic containers have self-locking vented lids with handles and are very inexpensive. A small box measuring 9.2 in x 6 in x 7 in / 23.36 cm x 15.24 cm x 17.78 cm retails for approximately $7 / £4.28.

Line the bottom of the box with some coconut fiber, which you can use as a substrate in the crabs' main habitat. Twenty-four quarts / 22.71 liters of this material costs about $17-$20 / £10.25-£12.

On the trip home, don't let the crabs get cold. Just putting them in an air-conditioned car could be too much stress, but excessive heat is just as bad. Take precautions in either case, protecting them from blasts of cold air or insulating the travel crate with your coat if it's winter time.

Make sure the travel container stays completely level for the ride home. If possible, take someone with you to the store who can hold the travel box for the ride home.

New Hermie on the Block

If you are adding a new hermit crab to an existing population, it's a good idea to place the new arrival in an isolation tank for 10 days to two weeks. This will ensure that the new hermit is disease and parasite free, and will also allow the crab to recover from the move and be in good shape to meet his new roommates.

You can expect some minor displays of territoriality from your existing crabs. It can be helpful to bathe all of the crabs in the same water to make sure there are no different smells in the crabitat. This precaution, plus having plenty of extra shells should allow everyone to be on good terms in fairly short order.

Chapter 3 - Hermit Crab Care

When you have made the decision to keep hermit crabs, you will want to prepare their environment in advance of the hermies' arrival in your home. Most of the supplies you need will be located in the reptile section of your big box pet store.

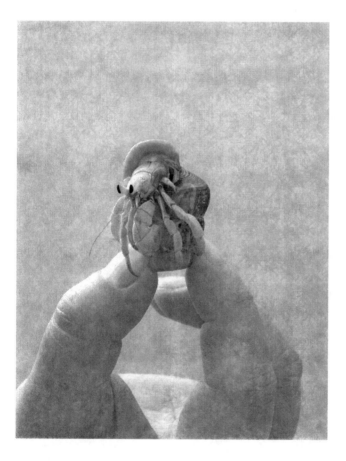

Obviously hermies aren't reptiles, but they are primarily housed in glass tanks, and they have similar needs for heat and humidity. This is actually to your benefit. Your store may not have a specific "hermit crab" aisle — in fact it probably won't, but you will still be able to get everything you need with very little trouble.

The more experienced you become, and if you decide to add more hermies to your population in the future, you may find that you can get your supplies at better prices online.

Designing Your Crabitat

Approach the design of your crabitat from the mindset of a world builder. You're not putting together some sort of "cage" for your pets. You're designing the place where they will live, "work," and play.

In their mind, their crabitat really is their whole world, and it should mimic, so closely as is possible, all the things they would enjoy if they were living in the wild on a shoreline, absent predators and all the other challenges they would face there.

As a beginning hermit crab keeper, a 10-gallon / 37.9 L aquarium is an excellent first crabitat. A standard tank of this size will measure:

20 inches / 50.8 cm long
10 inches / 25.4 cm wide
12 inches / 30.5 cm tall

The general rule of thumb is to allow 1.5 gallons / 5.7 L of space per 1 inch / 2.5 cm crab. So, in a 10-gallon / 37.9 L tank, you can easily keep six one-inch / 2.5 cm crabs or three two-inch / 5.1 cm crabs.

You not only need room for your hermies to move around, but you also need adequate space for all the things that will make their lives interesting and comfortable.

The Isolation Tank

In the previous chapter, I talked about buying a plastic "critter keeper" to bring your hermit crabs safely home. These plastic containers with self-locking vented lids are inexpensive and can be used as isolation tanks with one important qualifier.

A plastic box will work perfectly well as an isolation tank if you can maintain the correct temperature and humidity levels. If, however, you live in a climate where an under-the-tank heater is a necessity, the plastic may not be able to withstand the heat and a second 10-gallon / 37.9 L aquarium with its own heating pad will be required.

Positioning the Crabitat

Remember that hermit crabs come from a tropical environment so there are several things you want to avoid on both ends of the temperature extreme.

You certainly don't want the crabitat in a draft from a door, window, or AC vent. By the same token, you don't want it in direct sunlight or near heating vents.

As I mentioned in the Pros and Cons section of Chapter 1, a bedroom is not an ideal location because hermit crabs are nocturnal.

While you're trying to sleep, they'll be up playing, moving things around, and eating. They will make more noise than you think they will!

Temperature Control

The idea temperature for hermies is 72-78 °F / 22.2 C-25.5 °C. This is best maintained with an under tank heater, a device that looks like a heating pad. Don't use a heating pad or an electric blanket designed for humans. Both can overheat the interior of the tank.

Just because your hermit crabs want to live in a tropical environment doesn't mean you want to turn your house into a sauna. It is too difficult to try to control the climate in the crabitat by adjusting your own.

Under tank heaters designed for use with aquariums are just large enough to cover half of the tank, allowing your pets to choose between a "cool side" and a "warm side."

You can control the level of warmth on the heated half with the depth of substrate that you provide. Measure the internal temperature on the warm side to make sure you're not exceeding the recommended 72-78 °F range.

Don't buy any other heat product for your hermies like hot rocks or overhead reptile lamps. The under tank heater is all you will need. Any additional heat source will only cause the tank to dry out.

Humidity Control

Hermit crabs have gills like fish even though they don't live underwater. Their gills still have to be kept moist. Dehydration is a leading cause of death among captive hermit crabs, especially if they are allowed to escape their crabitat.

You need to keep the interior relative humidity of their crabitat at 70%-80%. For this reason, I recommend buying a thermometer / hygrometer combination so you can easily monitor both temperature and humidity.

These combination units generally cost $5-$10 / £3-£6.

Personally, I'm a fan of digital climate control like Fluker's Digital Display Thermo-Hygrometer for $20 / £12. The unit is easily read and shows both Celsius and Fahrenheit. It also is compact so it doesn't detract from the appearance of the crabitat and has a closure that is self-fastening.

From the instant your crabs come in the house, get in the habit of checking the humidity at least daily — or every time you walk by the crabitat!

Natural Sea Sponge

Keep a minimum of one natural sea sponge in the crabitat to help add moisture, but use more if necessary. Each sponge will cost $2-$5 / £1-£3. To get one that is really useful in a 10-gallon / 37.9 L aquarium, it will need to be roughly the size of a tennis ball or larger.

First, rinse the sponge in de-chlorinated water. You don't want any chemicals or residue that might create toxic fumes in the tank or that would encourage your hermies to start chewing on the sponge.

Either put the sponge directly in your crab's water bowl or get a second small bowl exclusively for the sponge. Monitor the sponge carefully to guard against growth of mold and bacteria, and always have an extra on hand so you can replace a bad sponge immediately.

If water droplets form on the side of the habitat, you need to bring the humidity level down, likely by lowering the interior temperature and perhaps removing the sponge for an hour or so. Continue to monitor both temperature and humidity until both levels are in the correct range.

Lighting

During the day, the available light in the room will work fine for your hermit crabs. Don't put a heating lamp on their tank, and don't "spotlight" them at night just so you can watch them.

If your crabs are most active in the evening and you want to enjoy their antics, use a lamp outfitted with a moonglow lightbulb costing $7-$10 / £4-£6.

This soft lighting will let you watch what your pets are doing, and it will mimic the natural light they'd experience during nocturnal beach scavenging.

Bedding or Substrate

Substrate serves a greater purpose than just giving your pets something other than a bare surface to walk on. Hermit crabs love to dig and tunnel.

The depth of the substrate should be twice as great as your largest crab. Shoot for roughly 3-5 inches / 7.6-12.7 cm for average size crabs and as much as 10 inches / 25.4 cm if you are keeping a larger species.

Plain sand and/or coconut fiber are considered the standard choices. Fine playground sand works quite well and is cheap at $6 /£3.67 per 50 lbs /22.7 kg.

Coconut fiber has the advantage of adding moisture without developing mold growth. The crabs' feces will naturally decompose in the fiber, so it will last a long time. The bedding does have to be misted to prevent drying, but it is still a low maintenance material.

Twenty-four quarts of coconut fiber retails for $17-$20 / £10.25-£12.

Substrates to Avoid

There are several materials that are not appropriate for use with hermit crabs. Wood shavings absorb too much moisture, and both pine and cedar emit phenols that are toxic to hermit crabs.

Cat litter is completely inappropriate. Crabs hate the texture and they have a tendency to try to eat the material, which can kill them.

Other types of bedding that are not right for your hermies include:

- potting soil
- paper towels
- newspaper
- ground walnut shells
- ground coconut shells

Collecting Beach Sand

While it is possible to collect free sand on the beach, it must be cleaned before use with your hermies. If you decide to go this route, get the sand as close to the waterline as possible.

Try to find sand that is reasonably dry. Sift through the material as you scoop it to remove large bits of foreign matter like shell fragments and rocks.

At home, spread the sand out on a clean baking sheet and put it in a 350 °F oven for 35-40 minutes. This will both dry the sand and kill any kind of parasites or pests living in it including mites and sand fleas.

While the sand is in the oven, stir it from time to time to ensure even heating and drying. Allow the sand to cool for at least 2 hours before putting it in the crabitat.

Adding Shelters

Remember that hermit crabs are nocturnal. During the day they like to hide in various kinds of shelters. You can get extremely creative with the "caves" you give your hermies. And if you're not creative, the people who design pet paraphernalia will do it for you!

Half coconut shells and hollowed out logs make good crab "shacks" and sell for $15 / £9.19 to $20 / £12.25 each. You will want at least one per crab.

Food and Water Dishes

Your crabs will need at least three bowls. One for fresh water, one for salt water, and a food dish. Go with a dish made of resin or strong plastic. Don't use anything metallic or porous.

Make sure the dishes are shallow enough for the crabs to get in and out. Obviously, if you have several crabs you will either need to buy large dishes, or provide several of each.

Always watch for signs of bullying. Sometimes larger individuals will keep their smaller roommates from getting enough to eat and segregated dining will be a necessity.

Since the crabs' water bowls will also double as their baths, the dishes should be big enough for the largest resident of the crabitat to fit into shell and all with 0.25 inches / 0.64 cm space on all sides and a water depth of 0.50 inches / 1.27 cm.

Don't give your crabs water any deeper than 0.50 inches / 1.27 cm or smaller crabs will drown. Keeping a sponge in the water dishes is a good safeguard. It gives the crabs a way to crawl out of the water.

Always use dechlorinated water. You can treat tap water with conditioners available at your pet store. Look for a product like Seachem Prime Water Conditioner that is appropriate for both fresh and salt water. A 100 ml bottle costs $3.75 / £2.29.

Saltwater for Your Hermies

Since hermit crabs would have access to saltwater in the wild, they need a dish in their crabitat. You must not use plain table salt to create their mini "ocean" however. First dechlorinate the water you intend to use, then add in a sea salt mixture as per the mixing instructions on the packaging.

Since these products are designed for enthusiasts keeping big saltwater tanks, you'll have to buy a large amount. Your choice of product may boil down to the one available in the smallest size.

Sea salt is often described in terms of how much water it will create by aquarium size. Often the smallest size you can buy is appropriate for a 50 gallon / 189.3 L tank and will cost approximately $15-$20 / £9.19-£12.25.

You will have to figure out the math to bring down the amount of water you are creating. For instance, if the product says to add 0.50 cup / 0.12 L per gallon, that's equal to 8 tablespoons / 120 g. Therefore:

0.50 gallon / 1.89 L = 4 tablespoons / 60 g
1 quart / 0.95 L = 2 tablespoons / 30 g
1 pint / 0.47 L = 1 tablespoon / 15 g
1 cup / 0.24 L = 0.5 tablespoon / 7.5 g

Once you figure out the formula for the sea salt mixture, write it down! I promise, you will not remember the next time you need to make another batch.

Decorating the Crabitat

One of the delightful things about keeping hermies as pets is how busy they are. It almost seems as if they wake up with an agenda on their minds and set about ticking things off their "to do" lists.

Hermit crabs spend all of their time exploring. You will want to give your pets things to climb, places to hide, toys to shove around, and extra shells for that all important real estate shopping.

Pick artificial plants and vines that are safe for use in aquariums (they'll dig up and eat the real thing), and never hesitate to move things around and redecorate.

Unlike many pets, hermies like it when you mix up their environment and give them something new to check out and think about.

Good decorations for climbing include ramps and branches, ladders, hammocks — really anything that can be used to create different levels. Think in terms of a crabitat jungle gym. Pay attention to what your crabs seem to particularly enjoy and expand on ideas that work.

Your Hermie Shopping List

The following are the major items you will need to include on your hermit's shopping list. Acquire all of these items and have them in place before you bring your pets home.

10-gallon/ 37.9 L aquarium
$15-$20 / £9-£12

aquarium lid
$8-$10 / £3.8-£6

"critter keeper" travel / isolation
9.2 in x 6 in x 7 in / 23.4 cm x 15.2 cm x 17.8 cm
$7 / £4.25

sand
5 lb / 2.3 kg
$5-$7 / £3-£4.25

coconut fiber
24 quarts / 22.7 L
$17-$20 / £10.25-£12

fine playground sand
50 lb / 22.7 kg
$6 / £3.64

under the tank heater
$12-$15 / £7.2-£9

thermometer / hygrometer combo
$5-$10 / £3-£6

sea sponge
$2-$5 / £1-£3

water conditioner (dechlorinator)
100 ml bottle
$3.75 / £2.24

sea salt mix
$15-$20 / £9-£12

fresh water dish
$5-$7 / £3-£4.25

salt water dish
$5-$7 / £3-£4.25

flat dish or tray for food
$5-$7 / £3-£4.25

toys for climbing
$3-$5 / £1.8-£3 each

box for hiding
(remember to get one per crab)
$15-$20 / £9-£12

three extra snail shells per crab
$3-$5 / £1.8-£3 each

moonglow light (bulb)
$7-$10 / £4.25-£6

secondary isolation tank for molting crabs
10-gallon / 37.9 L aquarium or smaller
(molting crabs are not very active)
$15-$20 / £9-£12

Total:
$153.75-$204.75 /£94.20-£125.45

*Note that the total above represents the supplies to outfit a crabitat for one hermie. You will require multiples of several of the items on the list including hide boxes and climbing toys.

Consider Stressors and Toxins

In discussing the placement of the crabitat, I discussed the importance of keeping your hermit crabs out of drafts and uncontrolled heat sources and minimizing their exposure to constant noise, but there are other environmental stressors you must consider.

Don't Use Painted Shells

In keeping with the way many people dress their pets — tutus for poodles or sombreros for Chihuahuas, for instance — some people think they can "dress" their hermit crabs by painting their shells. Don't do it!

Painting a shell that is used by a hermit crab is a deadly practice. The paint will not adhere well as the crab moves in and out of the water. As the paint flakes off, the crab eats the flakes, thus ingesting chemicals that will significantly shorten its life.

By the same token, you should never use anything in the crabitat that will leach chemicals into the water or that will present a toxic hazard if the crab attempts to eat the item.

Remember, crabs are scavengers. In their active little minds, everything is potential food.

Pay Attention to Air Quality

Be cautious about the kinds of chemical products you use in the vicinity of the crabitat. This precaution extends to such items as:

- all types of cleaning products
- aerosol air fresheners
- hairspray

- flea and tick sprays for other pets
- cigarette smoke

If it is absolutely essential that any of these items be used in the same area, cover the tank or relocate it. Any of these chemicals or similar substances can seriously irritate a crab's gills, which are essential for good health.

Misting and Bathing

In order to help your crabs stay clean and to hydrate their bodies and gills, you should both mist and bathe your pets. This is a simple process. It creates a further bonding activity, and your crabs love it!

How to Bathe Your Crabs

Bathing your hermit crabs is really just an issue of letting them splash around in clean water for a few minutes and then dry off in a box lined with paper towels.

- Prepare a jug of lukewarm water that includes a few drops of Stress Coat water conditioner (16 ounces / 0.47 L for $6 / £3.67) to remove any chlorine. This protects your pet's gills from potential blistering and will help to heal damaged skin tissue. NOTE, use Stress Coat for bathing ONLY, not to condition drinking water.

- Use any non-metal bowl or dish large enough to serve as a bathtub.

- Make a drying-off area by lining a shoebox or larger cardboard box with paper towels.

- Pour 0.25 inch / 0.64 cm of lukewarm to tepid water into the bath and add your crabs. Put them in upside down and let them straighten themselves out, or let them wander around in the water on their own.

- Placing them in upside down will help to remove anything lodged in their shells like feces or substrate.

- After they've had their bath, hold them upside down to drain excess water out of their shells, and then let them run around in the drying-off box. If you put them back in the crabitat, they'll be coated in substrate in nothing flat.

I generally try to schedule bathing and drying off time to coincide with my weekly deeper cleaning of the crabitat. Without my hermies to "help," I can sift the substrate clean of debris, rearrange the toys and climbing features, and wash out the extra empty shells.

Misting Your Hermies

Misting your hermit crabs will keep them well hydrated in between baths. Just pick up any kind of mist bottle and keep it filled with dechlorinated water.

Remove your pets from the crabitat and put them in a safe location. As they wander around looking things over, lightly mist them. They'll just assume it's raining.

You don't want to do this in the crabitat because the misting will promote too much moisture, which can lead to the growth of mold or fungus. Plus, when the crabs are damp, the substrate will stick to their bodies.

Don't mist more than once a week. If your tank is on the higher end of the recommended humidity level, closer to 80%, you can mist less. However, hermies really enjoy going for their weekly walk in the rain!

Handling and Bonding

Plan to spend time each day handling your hermies in order to bond with them. You will quickly learn their individual personalities, and they will come to recognize you and look forward to the interaction.

Picking Up Your Hermies

Always wash your hands thoroughly before you handle your pets. Don't put on any lotion. Reach in and grasp the back of the crab's shell to pick him up. NEVER pick up a crab from the front.

Using the other hand, cradle the crab, lightly, closing your fingers around him so that he feels safe. Don't close your fist around the little creature as this will cause him to panic.

Don't be surprised if your hermie retreats a bit into his shell, especially if he's not quite used to being handled.

Active crabs should be immediately transferred to another surface so they won't squirm loose. He may even pinch you a little, but it's not a sign of aggression, just the crab steadying himself so he won't fall. He'll let go as soon as he relaxes.

Should a hermit latch on and refuse to let go, just mist him a bit with warm water or return him to the crabitat. As soon as he realizes he's back on his home turf, he'll relax.

Playing with Hermie

Once you're settled with the crab, allow him to explore by walking around on your hand. Let him feel comfortable with you. Earn his trust by being gentle and talking to him softly.

I have found that crabs respond very well to being spoken to. They do not like sudden movements or loud noises.

If a child is holding the hermit crab, be sure they understand that a pinch simply is a request to be left alone. In general, I don't think it's a good idea to let a child hold a hermie due to the risk of the little creature being dropped.

It's better for the child to be seated on a carpeted floor, a bed, or a sofa. Then, if the child becomes startled and drops the crab, there's a protective cushion on which hermie will land and only a few inches to fall.

By offering your hermit crabs small treats, and calling their names, you can entice them to come out of their shells when "called." Granted, there aren't a lot of "tricks" a hermit can perform, but they will become very responsive pets once they become used to you.

Chapter 4 - Feeding and Crabitat Maintenance

Hermit crabs are scavenging omnivores. On their native beaches, they'll eat anything they find interesting including wood, insects, carrion, grass, fruits, and vegetables.

Although your hermies will eat and be happy with many of the same foods you're buying for yourself, they do have some particular nutritional requirements.

Commercial Hermit Crab Foods

Including a commercial hermit crab food in your pet's diet will ensure that your hermies are getting the correct amount of vitamins, minerals, and protein. You want to find a brand that has few preservatives, but includes calcium and carotene.

Typically, commercial foods are packaged in pellet form, but if your crabs are very small, they may not be able to grasp the pieces well enough to get an adequate serving.

Some owners solve this problem by grinding the food, while others prefer to find a flaked mixture.

You will see some products that are meat based that come in cans for about $1.50 / £0.91 each.

Examples of commercial crab dry mixes include:

Hikari Tropical Crab Cuisine
1.8 ounce / 51 g package
$2.50-$5 / £1.53-£3.06

HBH Hermit Crab Variety Bites
2.25 ounces / 63.8 g
$4 / £2.45

FMR Land Hermit Crab Food
4 ounces / 113.4 g
$3.25 / £1.99

Fresh Foods

Since so much of our food supply is contaminated with fertilizers and pesticides, it's best to feed your hermies organic produce if possible. While these things aren't good for us, they're certainly not good for tiny hermit crabs!

As a special note, hermies love strawberries, but they are one of the most heavily chemically polluted of all the fruits, so it's best to purchase organic fruit or not include them in your pet's menu.

Acceptable vegetables for your pet include:

carrots
lettuce
all leafy green vegetables
celery

spinach
parsely
corn
sweet potatoes
broccoli

In the fruit category hermies like:

coconut
mango
papaya
apples
grapes
pears
blueberries
guava fruit
bananas
melons
oranges

As omnivores, hermit crabs are also meat eaters and are especially fond of:

chicken
dried shrimp
krill
sardines
blood worms
meal worms
all types of sea life

Special Treats

Since it's so much fun to watch hermit crabs use their pinchers to manipulate their foods, it's all too tempting to give them "treats" they should not have. There are, however, some things they can eat safely as extras, including:

peanut butter
various types of seeds
algae
eggs
popcorn
crackers
unsweetened cereals
rice cakes
oatmeal

Also, since crabs like foods rich in tannin, they will happily munch on tree bark and oak leaves.

Foods to Avoid

Just because your crabs WILL eat pretty much anything is no sign they SHOULD. Foods you will want to AVOID include:

- anything that is processed
- anything full of preservatives
- anything high in sugar
- anything high in salt

Basically, if it comes in a box, is full of chemicals, and is bad for you? It's bad for your hermit crabs.

Sources of Calcium

If you are feeding your hermit crabs a commercial diet in addition to fresh foods, they should be getting enough calcium. You can, however, provide them with a number of additional calcium sources including:

- A cuttlebone, which you can find in the bird section of the pet store for about $1 / £0.61. This is the internal skeleton of the cuttlefish and is used as a source of calcium for many small companion animals.

- Calcium supplements for reptiles, which are packaged in powdered form and can be added to other foods. Approximately 3 ounces / 85 g costs $3-$5 / £1.83-£3.06.

- Crushed oyster shells can be purchased at stores that carry products for the care of poultry. A five-pound / 2.27 kg bag self for approximately $15 /£9.19.

- Crushed coral aquarium gravel is also an edible source of calcium, but is often hard to find in small lots. If you don't mind buying 15 lb / 6.8 kg, it will cost around $10 / £6.12.

Or, if you eat a lot of eggs, boil, dry and crush the shells and add the material to your crab's food dish. You can also give your crabs leftover bones from your own cooking, but be sure to wash off any seasonings before you put the items in the crabitat.

Sources of Carotene

In addition to calcium, hermit crabs need carotene to maintain their coloration. This is a particular problem with Ecuadorian and Strawberry hermit crabs. Both will fade out when they become carotene deficient.

Make sure that your crabs get red, orange, and yellow vegetables as well as dried shrimp and even fish flakes that are color enhancing. Feed the carotene-rich vegetables several times a week, and add a carotene supplement at least once a week.

Zoo Med packages a Sun-Dried Red Shrimp food primarily as turtle nutrition, but it will work well for hermit crabs and is affordable at $7 / £4.28 per 5 ounces / 141.7 g.

MarineLand Color-Enhancing Tropical Flakes are more expensive at $15 for 7.76 ounces, but one container will last a very long time.

Feeding Times

As nocturnal foragers, crabs naturally begin to wake up and get active around sunset. This is the best time to set their scheduled feeding, and is typically pretty convenient for their humans who are getting home from work or just about to go out for the evening.

It's best to pick a time and stick with it. Hermies quickly learn their schedule and enthusiastically await the arrival of their supper, which is fun for you.

You can offer your crabs food every day, but don't be concerned if they don't take it. Hermit crabs often go as much as a week or even longer without eating.

You should, however, continue to offer them food, removing whatever is uneaten on a daily basis. Leaving food in the tank will lead to mold, which will make your hermies sick.

Given the small size of the crabs' mouths and stomachs, you don't need to give them much. Just watch how much your pets do and don't eat and adjust the provided portions accordingly.

Try starting with just a pinch of fruit, vegetables, and pellet food. If it all disappears overnight, feed them again the next day and add a little more food. At the point at which you find leftovers the next morning, you've found the correct maximum portion.

Don't underestimate your crabs' ability to be picky. If you keep offering them a particular kind of food, only to throw it away time and time again, your hermies are trying to tell you something!

Also, hermit crabs have a tendency to hide and hoard their food. Check potential hiding spots throughout the crabitat routinely to make sure spoiled food is not sprouting mold in some dark spot.

Use Handfeeding for Bonding

Handfeeding your crabs is a good way to bond with your pets and to monitor how much food they're actually consuming. Your crabs will need awhile to become completely comfortable with you, so be patient.

Make sure that you wash your hands and that they are free of soap residue and lotion. Talk to your crabs while offering them food and move very slowly.

Wave a small piece of food in front of the crab's claws. Don't be surprised if your pet touches the food with his antennules to get a taste of what you're offering. If he likes the item, he'll use his small claw to take an exploratory pinch.

From this point, he may examine the food before bringing it to his mouth or spitting it out. He may also take the food and then very firmly push you away!

Hydration is Crucial

While a plentiful supply of clean, chlorine-free water is essential for all pets, your hermit crabs will die very quickly without it.

Your hermies don't just need water to drink, they need it to breathe. If their gills are not kept moist at all times, your pets will die.

Please see the previous chapter to understand how to bathe and mist your hermies. These husbandry activities are a necessary corollary to providing your crabs with fresh and saltwater dishes.

Crabitat Maintenance

Although the crabitat is easy to keep, you will have to commit to about 15 minutes of daily chores on behalf of your pets.

Hermies don't smell, but they do sometimes bury food and forget to go back and eat it later, leaving you to deal with a moldy mess.

For this reason, you need to inspect the crabitat every day for any little "treasures" your hermies have decided to store up for another day.

The major rule of crabitat care is NEVER use any soaps or cleaning products. The residue and fumes left by harsh chemicals will cause your hermies to sicken and die.

The following daily routine should allow you to quickly and efficiently keep your crabitat in good shape:

- Locate and remove all uneaten food.

- Rinse out all of the bowls with plain water and wipe them with paper towels.

- Refill the water bowls.
- Squeeze out the sea sponge and rinse it with dechlorinated water. The sponge should smell fresh before it's returned to the tank.

- If you can't get the sponge clean, let it dry completely and then microwave it for two minutes. Don't microwave a wet sponge or you'll ruin it.

- Shake out the extra shells so they're not filled with substrate. Add or switch out shells as needed.

- Inspect each crab for signs that they are about to molt. (See Chapter 5 on health to learn more about molting.) Crabs that are ready to molt will need to be moved to the isolation tank.

On a monthly basis, you will want to deep clean the habitat. Again, while your hermies are drying out from a bath is an excellent time to attend to maintenance issues.

- Take everything out of the crabitat and clean it all with a mixture of equal parts hot water and vinegar. Scrub all the toys and furnishings, and the food and water dishes.

- All wooden items should be placed in the microwave for a couple of minutes, and the extra shells should be boiled and allowed to cool.

- If you are using coconut fiber for bedding, remove the top 1 to 2 inches, turn over the remainder, and add more material as needed.

- If you are using sand, sift it to remove accumulated debris, then spread it out on a clean cookie sheet and bake it for 30 minutes at 350 °F / 176.7 °C for sterilization and drying. Make sure the substrate is completely cool before putting your pets back in the crabitat.

(It's also a good idea to keep two equal amounts of sand and always have a clean batch ready to go into the tank so your pets don't have to wait for "room service" to be done.)

- Dry the whole tank carefully with paper towels and, if possible, let the crabitat air outside in the sun.

Don't put anything new in the tank until you're sure it's clean and free of any potential toxic chemicals or fumes.

Chapter 5 - Health, Behavior, and Breeding

With good care, your hermit crabs can easily live 10 years. They are not the kind of pets you'll take to the vet on a regular basis, but there are potential health "issues" of which you should be aware.

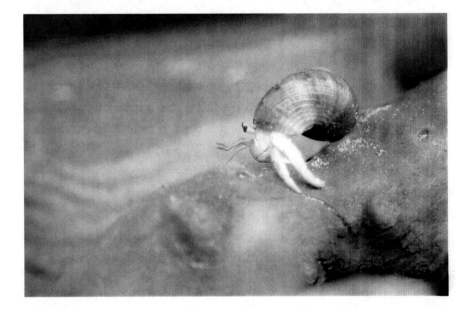

Signs of a Healthy Hermit Crab

The same standards you applied to picking a healthy hermit crab in the store should also be applied to observing your pets at home.

Healthy crabs:

- are active and curious
- live in clean shells that are intact with no damage
- don't hang out of the shell with a dried look

- are not being harassed by any parasites or insects
- have no strong odor

Preventive "Medicine"

The best way to ensure that your crabs are healthy is to provide them with good preventive "medicine," which means:

- well planned and maintained housing
- varied and nutritional food
- plentiful and clean fresh and saltwater
- access to additional shells in varying sizes

They also need to be protected from a variety of potential stresses including, but not limited to:

- constant loud noise
- aggression from tank mates
- toxins in the environment including insecticides
- forceful removal from their shells
- extremes and/or fluctuations in temperature and humidity
- bright lights
- poor quality water
- inadequate food
- no place to hide
- scarce or inappropriate selection of shells

A dirty substrate harboring insect life and fostering mold, bacteria, or fungal growth is extremely unhealthy.

Understanding Molting

All hermit crabs go through molting, which is the process of shedding an old exoskeleton for a new one for the purpose of growing larger.

This process can also accomplish regeneration from injuries. If, for instance, a crab has lost a limb or an antenna in an altercation with a tank mate, those appendages will grow back. Molting can even repair missing eyestalks.

In fact, examining a crab's injuries is a good way to determine if your pet is getting ready to molt. If he is, he'll excrete a clear gel from the end of the damaged body part.

Typically, older hermies molt once or twice a year, while smaller individuals go through the process multiple times over a single 12-month period.

Really, all a hermit crab needs for a successful molt is quiet time in an isolation cage where he can rest in private.

Other signs of an impending molt include:

- Digging around in the crabitat looking for an isolated spot to bury himself.

- Eating or drinking more than usual to store up energy for the molting process.

- Markedly decreased activity to the point of immobility, with drooping antennas and dull, clouded eyes.

When you realize that a crab is about to molt, bathe your pet in lukewarm water mixed with Stress Coat. The additional moisture will help the molting process get started. After the hermit is dry, transfer it to an isolation tank that includes 6 inches /15.2 cm of sand.

The temperature in the isolation tank should be about 76 °F / 24.4 °C with 70% relative humidity. Lightly mist the isolation tank each day in the general vicinity of where the crab has buried himself.

There's no need for any furnishings or climbing toys, but the crab will need the usual fresh and saltwater dishes and some extra shells. The tank should be kept in a dark, quiet spot with low traffic.

The crab will bury himself deep in the sand and may not emerge again until he's finished molting. Very rarely, a hermie will molt on the surface. If that happens, just leave your pet alone. He knows what he's doing. Do not mist crabs molting on the surface of the substrate.

The total length of the molting process should be no more than two weeks, although some crabs require an entire month.

Unexpected Molting

If you miss all of the signs of an impending molt and the crab has already buried himself in the substrate, isolate him from his tank mates with a tank divider.

If you don't know where the crab is located, don't go digging around in the substrate looking for him, but consider moving everyone else to another tank.

If you don't separate molting crabs from the rest of the population, the smell of the molting will cause the tank mates to turn cannibalistic.

If a crab begins to molt on the surface, gently remove him to the isolation tank by surrounding him with substrate and lifting him with a large spoon.

During and After the Molt

Hermits twist and stretch to break free of their old exoskeleton, which ultimately splits open and slips free. The fragments may remain in the crab's shell or fall out.

When the molting is finished, the crab will hide out to rest and recuperate. Because his new exoskeleton has not yet hardened, the crab is highly vulnerable.

He will eat the old exoskeleton as a way to reclaim the vitamins, minerals, and nutrients it contains. If the shell isn't available to him for whatever reason, make sure the freshly molted crab has a cuttlebone or some other source of calcium, which he especially needs at this time.

Otherwise, leave your pet alone until he resumes his previous level of activity. Do give him a good variety of fresh shells, which he'll enjoy trying on as soon as his new exoskeleton has hardened.

As soon as he's walking around again, he can be returned to the crabitat.

Molting Tragedies

Molting is a difficult process that leaves the crab stressed and highly vulnerable. It is possible for individuals that are not strong going into the molt to die during the process.

Crabs that bury themselves to molt and don't come up after a month, have likely died. Certainly if you begin to detect a bad odor emanating from the isolation tank, it's time to start gently moving the sand to the side to look for the hermie.

If he's still alive, cover him with a large shell, but don't put the dislodged substrate back in place since it could suffocate the molting crab.

If your pet has died, dispose of the remains and all of the substrate. Clean the tank thoroughly with hot water and vinegar and allow everything to air outside in the sun.

Understanding Normal Behavior

Since hermit crabs are not your usual run of the mill pets, first-time crab keepers have difficulty deciding what's normal for their hermies.

Crabs Make Noise

First, it's perfectly normal for hermit crabs to make noises to communicate with their roommates and with you. The technical term for their vocalization is "stridulation."

It sounds something like a cricket or a croaking frog. You'll hear a lot of this clicking and chirping when your hermies are awake and active. They'll make even more noise when they're annoyed, hurt, lost, scared, or happy.

When you pick up a crab, he'll usually make a sound. Don't assume this is fear or anxiety. He may just be glad to see you!

If you're doing something else near the crabitat and you hear multiple vocalizations going on for a fairly long period of time, go find out what's happening. You may be needed to break up a shell fight.

Ecuadorian hermit crabs are highly vocal, as are *C. rugosus*, known as "ruggies." They make so much noise they are sometimes referred to as "crying crabs."

Wrecking the Crabitat

Every night your hermies will wake up, have a bite to eat, and then get down to "work." All night long, as they go about socializing and playing, your pets will pretty much trash the place.

The next morning you'll find all the toys moved, the plastic plants knocked over and dragged about, and the substrate thoroughly rearranged. Expect flipped over dishes and general mayhem.

What does this mean? The hermies had a great party and would like you to please put everything back where it was so they can do it all over again the next night.

Wrestling and Game Play

Many people are shocked at just how rowdy a tank full of hermies can be. They love to wrestle, and will blatantly crawl right over another crab that has gotten in the way.

You'll look into the crabitat and find a pair dueling with their antennae, or fencing and pinching at one another with their claws.
Most of this behavior is simple roughhousing to pass the time. If you really see a couple of hermit crabs fighting, you'll know it.

Aggression and Fighting

Some crabs, when confined to a crabitat, don't get high marks for playing well with others. For the most part, hermies go about their own business, but they can get in a bad mood, suffering stress from:

- overcrowding
- being the new kid on the block
- poor handling

As a result, you can wind up with a real bully that takes food away from his roommates or prevents them from using the water bowl. Aggressive crabs get highly territorial and sometimes just downright mean.

This is when you start to see behaviors like shell stealing, an activity that, while it sounds amusing, can actually represent a blood feud that ends not just in eviction but death.

When you see two crabs behaving aggressively and fighting, remove the aggressor. If the fight appears to have been over a shell, offer him a similar shell. Hopefully, he'll move in assuming he's the victor and the matter will be over.

It is possible, however, for two crabs to simply take a dislike to one another that necessitates they be separated permanently.

Always ask to handle crabs before you buy them. Any crab that tries to pinch the palm of your hand in the store will likely exhibit aggression in the crabitat.

Hermie Seems Withdrawn

Occasionally, the problem behavior isn't that your crab is aggressive, but rather that it is withdrawn, hiding in its shell, and refusing to come out.

Withdrawn hermit crabs may also bury themselves for days on end, or refuse to leave their hideouts. There are many things that may lead to this kind of behavior.

Crabs who have just had their shell stolen will often retreat from the world, as will those that are being bullied and driven away from food and water.

Often a hermit new to the crabitat will withdraw temporarily, but should improve over a period of days.

Any time a crab is behaving in a shy and withdrawn manner offer him more food, water, and treats as well as a bigger choice of shells. Keep the area adjacent to the crabitat quiet and be on the lookout for signs of aggression or bullying that may be upsetting the hermit.

Withdrawing is often a problem in Ecuadorian crabs. They may become so listless and apathetic they refuse to eat and will slowly starve. For this reason, it is always best to keep at least three Ecuadorian crabs together, which seems to help these sensitive creatures overcome their native shyness.

Dealing with Insects in the Crabitat

Unfortunately, your crabitat can be a real breeding ground for insects harmful to your hermit crabs. With the warmth of the enclosure, the humidity, and the deep substrate, all manner of bugs will find your hermies' home the perfect place to hide and help themselves to free food and water.

The insects that most typically set up shop in a crabitat include:

- mites
- flies
- fly larva
- ants

If you see small creatures that are white or brown and shaped like kernels of rice crawling on your hermies, you have an infestation of mites.

This or any type of insect activity must be addressed immediately before the bugs get inside your pet's shell and begin feeding off the crabs themselves as well as the food you provide for them daily.

Crabs that are infested with mites or pestered by any other kind of insects will become severely stressed, often lose limbs, stop eating, and may die.

Ants or flies are equally as dangerous as mites. If flies lay their eggs inside the crab's shell, the hatching larvae will feed on the crab's abdomen killing your pet in short order.

Combating Pests

To combat any pests that move into the crabitat, you must first remove your crabs and bathe them in a mixture of lukewarm saltwater.

Do not use table salt to prepare the bath. Always use marine salts. The iodine in table salt will kill your pets.

Any insects infesting your crabs will float to the surface of the bath water, so be sure to pour the dirty water out of the container while holding your crab. You don't want to lift him directly out of the water, or you'll just bring the insects back out with him.

Change the dirty water for clean water that includes a few drops of Stress Coat, and bathe your pets again. Then place them in a box lined with paper towels to air dry.

When they are dry, examine the crabs for any visible sign of insect activity. You may need to put your pets through three to four baths until the water comes up clean with no floating insects and none on the crabs themselves.

Clean and Disinfect the Crabitat

While your pets are drying, completely disassemble the crabitat and discard all of the old substrate. Give everything in the tank a good scrubbing with a mixture of hot water and vinegar at a 50/50 ratio.

Boil all of the extra shells for 2-5 minutes, rinsing them and allowing them to drain and cool.

Get rid of the existing sea sponges and replace them with new ones. Put any wooden toys or features in the microwave for 3 minutes or bake them in a 300 °F / 148.9 °C oven for half an hour.

Scrub all visible areas of the crabitat and allow it to air dry in the sun. Only reassemble the tank and reintroduce the crabs when you are sure both the enclosure and your pets are free of any pest presence.

What Attracted the Pests?

After you've dealt with an infestation of insects in the crabitat, try to figure out what happened.

- Have you been cleaning the crabitat daily?
- Are you removing all uneaten food?
- Do you need to consider a different substrate?
- Are you keeping the crabitat overly humid?
- Does the tank lid fit securely and is it undamaged?
- Are adjacent houseplants attracting insect life?
- Did the insects "ride along" with a newly acquired crab?

Even if you think your husbandry is excellent on all points, increase your level of vigilance. Take appropriate countermeasures.

If, for instance, you've had an issue with ants, smear a layer of petroleum jelly around the top 2 inches of the tank to trap the ants.

(Make sure your crabs can't come into contact with the substance since they will eat it and get sick.)

Breeding Hermies?

Breeding hermit crabs in captivity is neither a goal nor a worry. Hermies can't reproduce in their crabitat. They have to lay their eggs in the ocean.

The babies are born without shells and live by eating plankton. The necessary conditions can't be recreated by enthusiasts in a home setting.

Chapter 6 - Frequently Asked Questions

Although I suggest you read the entirety of this text to understand how to care for your hermit crabs, these are some of the most frequently asked questions about hermies.

How do you tell the gender of a hermit crab?

While it is not impossible to determine the gender of your hermit crabs, it can only be done when they are out of their shells. It is imperative, however, that you never force a crab to come out of its shell.

Also, when hermies are kept as pets, gender really does not matter. There is no personality difference, and your crabs cannot breed in captivity.

If, however, you are curious, female crabs have no gonopores, or genital openings on the top part of their back walking legs. These orifices are very small and difficult to see. During mating, males insert their spermatophores in the female's gonopores.

Why can't hermit crabs be bred in captivity?

In communities of hermit crab keepers, there is always someone who insists that hermies can be bred in captivity. It is more accurate to say that your female crabs may produce eggs, but those eggs will not survive.

Female hermit crabs lay their eggs and then carry them to the ocean to release them on the retreating tide. The young crabs live on plankton until they are old enough to return to the shore. In the absence of access to the open ocean, hermit crabs cannot complete their reproductive cycle.

What is the purpose of keeping extra shells in a crabitat?

Hermit crabs grow by a process of molting. They shed their old exoskeleton and form a new one that is just a little larger each time. Your hermies will want a new shell to move into that fits properly. On average, the crabs molt every 10-18 months.

That's the practical side to the business of extra shells. The truth is that hermit crabs just love to shop for new homes. Often they change shells just to try out a new "house" while still holding on to the old one with one leg.

Shell fights are not unusual, nor is "buyer's remorse." A crab may stay in a new shell for a few hours and then go right back to the old one. Don't try to figure out why. I think they just do it because they can.

Is play sand okay to use for a substrate in my crabitat?

Many people do use play sand, but it's not my personal favorite as a substrate. I prefer coconut fiber because it lasts longer and the crab's feces naturally decompose in the material.

Do hermit crabs carry any disease?

No, hermit crabs do not carry any known disease. It's a myth that hermit crabs can carry salmonella. That is a problem for people with pet reptiles, but not for people who have hermies.

If they don't carry any disease, is it necessary to wash my hands after I handle them?

You should wash your hands before and after you handle your hermit crabs. It's not so much a matter of your health as theirs! Certainly, you can come away from handling your crabs with bits of dirt and substrate on your hands.

Crabs are diggers, after all, but the crabs can come away with all kinds of residue from your skin as well. The safest course for all concerned is to wash your hands before you handle the crabs, but make sure you are completely free of chemical residue or lotions. After you've handled your pets, wash your hands thoroughly in hot, soapy water.

Is it a good idea to paint a hermit crab's shell or not?

You will certainly see people selling painted shells for use with hermit crabs. They might be cute, but don't go there. Nature offers far too many interesting and appropriate shells for use with your pets.

Don't buy painted shells, and don't paint your own even if you think you're using non-toxic paint. Ultimately, your crabs will eat the paint that flakes off and it's not healthy for them.

Will insects be attracted to the crabitat?

Often, both gangs and mites are attracted to even the cleanest of crabitats due to the moisture and the presence of organic substrate. You will have to completely sterilize the tank to get rid of these unwelcome guests, a process I discuss in the chapter on hermit crab health.

My crab is very shy. Is there anything I can do to encourage him to be more social?

Never force a hermit crab to come out of his shell. Your pet may be experiencing stress, or he could even be tired. Remember, hermies are nocturnal, so if you try to get him up in the day, he isn't going to be happy.

You can try to entice a crab to come out of his shell by softly blowing on him, or you can lightly mist your pet. If he still doesn't respond, leave the crab alone. The more you annoy him, the more stressed he will become.

One of my crab's front pinchers is bigger than the other one. Why?

It's perfectly normal for one of your hermit crab's front pinchers to be larger than the other. That's the way nature designed him!

When I try to hold my hermie he pinches me. Why?

Hermit crabs are scavengers, and curious by nature. They'll try to pinch whatever is available just to check it out. When you allow your pet to explore your hand, hold the skin taut so there are no loose folds to attract his attention.

If you have a crab that isn't used to you yet and pinches you every time, only hold your pet over a soft surface. If you get startled and drop your pet on a hard surface from a standing height, the result could be tragic.

Over time, your hermie should get used to you and stop the pinching behavior. If he doesn't, you may have an individual that is simply aggressive by nature.

I've started to notice a fishy, musty smell coming from my crabitat. What's going on?

It's very possible that one of your crabs has died. Look first to see if any of your crabs is showing a brown discharge. This is a sign of death by overheating. Are any of your crabs missing? One may have buried himself to molt and not survived the process. Begin gently moving aside the substrate to see if you can locate the crab.
In either case, it's best to relocate all your crabs to the isolation tank, wash everything in the crabitat with a 50/50 solution of water and vinegar, and completely replace the substrate.

I've been told that keeping only one crab is a bad idea. Why?

Hermit crabs are social animals. In the wild, they travel in groups of as many as 100. If kept alone in captivity, loneliness will shorten your pet's life.

It's always best to keep as many hermit crabs as you can manage. They'll be much happier, and the maintenance profile does not increase significantly with multiple pets.

How many hermit crabs should I keep?

The rule on number of crabs is dependent on the space you have for a good crabitat. The standard "rule" is to figure 1.5 gallons / 5.67 L of space per 1 inch / 2.54 cm crab.

Therefore, in a 10-gallon / 37.85 L tank, you could keep six one-inch / 2.54 cm crabs or three two-inch / 5.08 cm crabs. It is important that the living space not be cramped and that the crabs can move around without crawling all over one another.

How big should my crabs' habitat be?

The best advice I can offer anyone in designing any type of habitat for a companion animal is to get the largest enclosure you can afford and position in your home. With hermit crabs, I recommend a 10-gallon / 37.85 L aquarium.

That size allows for plenty of room for the crabs and for all the things they need to be happy and healthy, including food, water bowls, and toys.

Do hermit crabs produce feces?

Of course they do, but they have something of a system about handling it all. The feces collect in their shells, and periodically the crab scoops it all out. You may never even see the feces in the substrate, but you still have to change the material out completely on a monthly basis.

Even though the crab scoops its own "poop," you still have to bathe your pets weekly. If you don't, a lot of unhealthy dirt and grime will build up inside their shells.

Do hermit crabs need special lighting?

Hermit crabs are nocturnal and they don't like a lot of bright light. Just normal daylight room light is fine. You can use a moon glow bulb in a reptile light at night if you want to watch your pets without bothering them. NEVER use a heating lamp with your hermies.

I'm seeing some crusty deposits around my crab's eyes. What is it?

Often crabs will develop a crusty substance around their eyes just before they get ready to molt. This is a good sign that you may need to move hermie to the isolation tank.

Are there any good ways to socialize a hermit crab?

You have to understand that hermit crabs actually do have very distinct personalities all their own. Some will be social, some will not.

You'll stand a better chance of having happy crabs that want to interact if you keep several, but even then, some just won't be the life of the party. Accept each crab for what it is and enjoy each individual's natural style of being "crabby."

Does a hermit crab digging indicate he's about to molt?

Digging behavior may indicate molting, or the crab may just be doing what he does naturally. Sometimes crabs will also dig if they are too warm or too cold.

How often should my crabitat be cleaned?

Hermit crabs produce very little waste, allowing for once a week cleaning with more extensive maintenance monthly and complete substrate changes every six months.

In Chapter 4 on feeding and maintenance, I suggest a schedule for given cleaning chores to keep your hermies in top shape.

Do hermit crabs bite?

Hermit crabs don't have teeth, so they can't bite. They will use their pinchers to test out things, including the palm of your hand or your fingers as potential food. They will also pinch you if they feel defensive.

How big will my hermit crab grow?

That depends on species and how long your crab lives in captivity, which can be as much as ten years. It's not unusual for a well-cared for crab to grow to roughly the size of a baseball.

Why aren't my crabs more active during the day?

Hermit crabs are nocturnal. Your pets will start to get more active around dusk, and putter around in their crabitat all night. Leave them alone during the day, and they'll get up sooner at night.

You can also install a moon glow bulb in a lamp over the crabitat to get a better view of them in dim light. Never, however, use a heating lamp with your pets.

Also, remember that each crab has a unique personality. Some will actually be active during the day. The best thing to do is simply to let your crabs be what they are going to be.

I am personally against trying to alter a creature's natural life rhythms, but some people do increase the crabitat temperature to a range of 75-85 °F / 23.9-29.4 °C and mist daily to get their crabs to be more active in the daytime.

I'm seeing a kind of oily residue in the bottom of my crab's dishes. What is it?

The residue could be either bacterial growth or the oil left behind by some commercial crab foods. Use a damp paper towel to clean the dish, but don't use any soap. If the substance is really stubborn, use a 50/50 solution of water and vinegar, but be sure to rinse the dish thoroughly.

If my crab is dropped, will it survive?

It's extremely important that you protect your crabs from being dropped or falling onto hard surfaces during times when they are roaming free, especially if you have them on a table top.

Due to the location and design of their eyes, hermies can't look down and will walk straight off the edge of a table. If a crab falls onto a hard surface from even a small distance, it can sustain fatal injuries.

When I approach my hermit crabs, they duck back into their shells. Am I doing something to scare them?

Your crabs aren't used to you yet. Any sudden movement or even a shadow falling over the crabitat will startle them, especially if they are new to the environment. Move slowly and carefully, and speak softly to your pets. They will get used to you in time and stop ducking into their shells.

One of my hermit crabs lost a limb. Should I do anything to help him?

No. There's no reason to panic. It's common for crabs to lose limbs, and it may even have occurred naturally rather than as a result of aggression in the tank. During your pet's next mold, the limb will grow back. There's nothing you need to do to help your pet.

Why do hermit crabs sometimes lose their legs?

If your hermit crab has lost a leg, it is possible that the crabitat is too dry, or that it is not being cleaned often enough.

It's important that your crab have access to water-filled sponges in their water dish, that they have a source of saltwater, that they are misted routinely, and bathed weekly.

While the missing limb will regenerate during the next molt, the fact that it did fall off is a good indication that you need to reassess your level of husbandry for your pets.

Please see Chapters 3 and 4 for more information on daily care and feeding of your pets and on crabitat design and maintenance.

What are some of the reasons why a hermit crab will come out of his shell?

Hermit crabs will leave their shells if they have become too dirty, creating itchiness and irritation for the crab. If this is the case, the crab may permanently abandon the shell and look for a new one.

This is why it's important once a crab is settled in new quarters to boil the old shell for approximately two minutes to get it completely clean before returning it to the crabitat for use by other inhabitants.

Always boil shells in plain hot water. Never use any kind of cleaning agent, and make sure the shell is completely cool before putting it back in the crabitat.

It's also possible that the shell has developed a crack or a break. If this is the case, discard the shell and provide a new one of an equal or greater size.

What happens to my hermit crabs when they molt?

Hermit crabs shed their exoskeletons on a periodic basis so they can grow larger. Any damaged or missing body parts including eyes and claws will regenerate during this process.

While molting, crabs remain in their shells, but will probably bury themselves deep in the sand of their crabitat for days or weeks. This allows their vulnerable new skin to harden. So long as there is no foul odor in the tank, leave your pet alone during this time.

Because hermit crabs lose 90% of the calcium in their bodies during molting, they will eat their old exoskeleton to reclaim as much of the mineral as possible.

It's also a good idea to offer your crabs egg shells or cuttlebone as additional sources of calcium.

Molting crabs should be isolated in a separate tank so they can go through this process as quietly as possible and not be bothered by other tank mates.

How should I handle my hermit crabs to avoid getting pinched?

By nature, hermit crabs are passive and very easy to hold in the palm of your hand. If they pinch lightly, they're just looking around and being curious.

A more definite pinch may be because your crab is afraid, or because he's unsteady and is looking for something to hold on to.

Should a crab ever latch on to you and not let go, just gently mist him or place him under a stream of tepid water. He'll let go immediately.

Should your crab break the skin, which isn't likely, don't be concerned about infection. Hermit crabs don't carry any known disease. Just rinse out the spot with hydrogen peroxide to be on the safe side as you should with any small cut.

Should I handle my hermit crabs or just watch them?

You want to interact with your hermit crabs. Most of them like to be handled. They may be shy at first and have to get used to you, but once they are socialized, they'll look forward to seeing you.

As for watching their antics, hermies are curious, intelligent, and very busy. Your little friends will provide you with hours of entertainment.

Never try to force a crab out of his shell, however. They will literally allow themselves to be torn apart before they give up their homes!

Will hermit crabs reproduce in captivity?

Hermit crabs can't reproduce in captivity because they don't have access to the open ocean. Mother crabs deposit their eggs on the retreating tide. The eggs hatch in the water and survive in a planktonic state early in life. These conditions are almost impossible to reproduce in captivity, especially by a hobbyist crab keeper.

What are the major differences between Purple Pincher and Ecuadorian hermit crabs?

Purple Pincher or Caribbean Hermit Crabs (Coenobita clypeatus) and Ecuadorian Hermit Crabs (Coenobita compressus) are the two types of land crabs primarily sold as pets.

Purple Pinchers are found in the Caribbean and are nicknamed for their distinctive purple-colored large pincher. They drink fresh water (although they can consume saltwater) and they live inland.

The Ecuadorian Hermit Crab is a greenish blue, and turns orange and tan as they age. They live closer to the shoreline and need saltwater to drink. They do not have any distinctive coloration on their claws.

How long will my "hermies" live?

A hermit crab's average life span is 5-10 years, although many can live to 15 years. The oldest recorded age of a hermit crab kept in captivity is 40 years.

How can I get rid of mites inside the crabitat?

Mites can appear in crabitats where the environment is too humid or in instances when uneaten food is left in the cage too long. When mites are present, you should first remove your crabs and wash them in a bath of dechlorinated saltwater. This may require more than one treatment to get rid of all the mites.

Sterilize everything in the crabitat and clean everything with a lukewarm mixture of 50/50 dechlorinated water and vinegar. Boil everything in the cage for at least 2 minutes.

When everything is dry, put down completely fresh substrate.

Continue to watch for signs of mites and repeat maintenance and treatment as required.

Afterword

As I described in the foreword, my own hermies came to me basically through benevolent abandonment. My colleague and I have laughed about it since. He'll stick his head in my office and say, "How are *our* hermies?"

I think when he and his wife went off on vacation they knew what would happen. That I'd become fascinated by the little creatures, begin learning about them, and be perfectly happy for them to stay. He was right.

Having kept other small animals in aquaria and in small wire cages, I can truthfully say keeping a crabitat is much less work. Personally, I use coconut fiber because the crab's feces naturally decompose in the material.

I do have to mist the fiber to keep the humidity level up, but that's nothing. The crabs seem to think they're getting their own personal little rain storm and appear to enjoy it very much.

When people see the crabitat and exclaim about the pretty shells I've provided for my pets, I tell them it's a matter of "Lifestyles of the Rich and Crab Famous." I think my hermies appreciate the fact that I go a bit above and beyond on shell selection.

Recently, a friend who is a shell collector commented that I do basically the same thing, but mine walk around all the time! Actually my crabs, who are all Purple Pinchers, don't just walk around, they scurry about, rearrange their furniture, climb endlessly, and love to play in their water dishes.

I'm lucky. We don't have issues of aggression over shell changes, but I've read stories on forums of hermies that have become so obsessed with reclaiming a shell they unwisely abandoned that they essentially commit crabby murder to get it.

I always tell people who are new to this enthusiasm not to underestimate the level of aggression a hermit crab can display. They will, literally, rip each other's legs off. Of course, if the crab survives, the legs will grow back during the next molt, but all too often, these neighbor wars are duels to the death.

Although I didn't set out to become a crab keeper, I'm not at all sorry to have my little friends. I do suggest that you not only read this book, but also visit some hermit crab discussion forums online like those at The Hermit Crab Addiction at TheHermitCrabAddiction.net to really get a feel for life with hermies.

If you choose to set up a crabitat and bring hermit crabs home, I think you'll find that your new pets afford you hours of pleasure and entertainment. I have to confess I sometimes start watching mine and realize I've let an hour or more pass.

Regardless, perhaps you will at least come away from this book with a new appreciation for hermit crabs, their intelligence, their personality, and the complexity of their interactions. They are far from simple little animals and they are certainly not "throw away" pets.

If you have the time and space to properly care for hermit crabs, and they are a good fit in your life, they will soon become a part of your life. I swear mine are glad to see me at the end of the day, and I know I'm glad to see them.

Relevant Websites

General Information

Absolutely Crabulous
http://www.absolutely-crabulous.co.uk

The Crabstreet Journal
crabstreetjournal.org

Best Fiddler Crab Care
http://www.freewebs.com/fiddlercrabcare/

Embrace the Random
The Care and Maintenance of Fiddler Crabs
aquilusdomini.blogspot.co.uk/2012/08/the-care-and-maintenance-of-fiddler.html

The Fiddler Crab, Uca pugnax
http://www.vims.edu/~jeff/fiddler.htm

Practical Fishkeeping
Fiddler Crabs
http://www.practicalfishkeeping.co.uk/content.php?sid=312
0

Best Fiddler Crab Tank Mates: What Fish Can Live with My
Fiddler Crab?
voices.yahoo.com/best-fiddler-crab-tank-mates-fish-live-with-3798004.html?cat=53

Relevant Websites

Mini Crabs as Pets
http://www.dfs-pet-blog.com/2011/01/fiddler-crabs/

Hermit Crab Association
http://www.hermitcrabassociation.com

Hermit Crab Species Identification
http://www.hermit-crabs.com

Live Hermit Crabs
http://www.livehermitcrabs.com

The Crabstreet Journal
http://www.crabstreetjournal.com

Pet Discounters
http://www.petdiscounters.com

Hermit Crabs
hermit-crabs.com

Hermit Crabs
hermitcrabs.org

Animal Planet - Hermit Crabs
http://www.animalplanet.com/marine-life/hermit-crab-info.htm

Land Hermit Crabs
http://www.landhermitcrabs.com

Hermit Crab Patch
http://www.hermitcrabpatch.com

Hermit Crab Paradise
http://www.hermitcrabparadise.com

The Hermit Crab Addiction
http://www.hermitcrabaddictionstore.com

Coenobita Species
http://www.coenobitaspecies.com

Unique Idea for Designing Your Crab Habitat

Atlantis Underwater Island
http://www.crabhomes.com/

Create an Underwater Dry Zone in Your Aquarium
lifehacker.com/5929789/create-an-underwater-dry-zone-in-your-aquarium

http://www.instructables.com/id/Under-water-Dry-zone-for-fiddler-crabs/

Videos

Fiddler Crab Waving display
http://www.youtube.com/watch?v=Gwet0JLuqWY

Fiddler Crabs - Filmed in Brooklyn, New York at low tide.
http://www.youtube.com/watch?v=93J5JC3JEuI

Fiddler Crab Molting

http://www.youtube.com/watch?v=_TihBgdoFBw

A Few Days in the Lives of My Fiddler Crabs

http://www.youtube.com/watch?v=qMkt2POLo_4

Making a Fiddler Crab Habitat

http://www.youtube.com/watch?v=QBN6atggUcw

Glossary

abdomen - In hermit crabs, the abdomen is the region of the body farthest from the mouth and before the animal's curving tail. It is extremely soft and vulnerable, which is why the crabs seek out snail shells to serve as protective coverings.

antennae - A crab's sense organs or feelers are his antennae. He uses them to both smell and taste. Your crab has two pairs of antennae, long and short, located at the front of his head.

antennule - These are a hermit crab's smaller antennae and are the foremost of the two pair.

cheliped - The word cheliped, which is pronounced "keel-i-pee" means "claw" and "foot." This refers to a crab's grasping claws or pinchers which are used to hold food, for climbing, and as a means of defense. Hermit crabs also use the larger of their two pinchers to measure the entrance of a new shell to make sure it will fit their bodies, and then to block the opening to the chill once they are inside.

chitin - Hermit crabs are arthropods. Like insects, they have exoskeletons made of chitin, which they shed in order to grow. The process by which the exoskeletons are exchanged is called molting. After the old shell is shed, the crab's epidermis secretes a new, larger exoskeleton that gradually hardens, but allows interior room for future growth.

Coenobita - The scientific name for the family of land-based or terrestrial hermit crabs.

crabitat - The common term to refer to the habitat in which pet hermit crabs live, typically, a 10-gallon / 37.85 L aquarium.

crustacean - A group of animals that are primarily aquatic in nature and include lobsters, crabs, shrimps, and prawns.

ecdysis - The proper name for the process by which a hermit crab and similar creatures shed their old exoskeleton and excrete a new one for the purpose of achieving growth.

hermie - The accepted and affectionate shorthand used by enthusiasts to refer to hermit crabs.

maxillipeds - A crab's maxillipeds are the small appendages near the mouth that serve as tiny "hands" for the purpose of taking food from the claws and bringing it to the mouth. The maxillipeds are also used in grooming.

molting - The process by which an organism sheds an old exoskeleton and excretes a larger one that hardens and allows room for internal growth. The process is also regenerative in nature since damaged body parts are typically reformed during this process.

nocturnal - Creatures that are nocturnal are more active at night and tend to sleep during the day. This is true of hermit crabs. Your hermies will tend to wake up around dusk and will play and scavenge through their crabitat all night.

setae - Long hairs growing between the joints of a crab's legs and on its maxillipeds. These are not "hairs" per se, but projections of the crab's exoskeleton. They are also sensory in function.

Index

abdomen, 19, 33

aggression, 32, 103

antennae, 18, 21, 22

aquarium, 1, 2, 27, 41, 42, 45, 50, 52, 54, 107

aquatic, 11, 12

breeders, 18

buying hermit crabs, 30

calcium, 60, 64, 65

calcium supplements, 64

Caribbean hermit crab, 16

carotene, 60, 65

cavipes, 18

chelipeds, 20

children, 22, 24

cigarette smoke, 56

claws, 12, 16, 18, 20

cleaning, 21, 55

commercial diet, 64

crabitat, 2, 15, 24, 26, 31, 36, 39, 41, 42, 44, 45, 46, 49, 50, 52, 54, 55, 65, 66, 102, 103

crabitats, 12

critter keeper, 37, 42, 52

crushed coral aquarium gravel, 64

crushed oyster shells, 64

crustaceans, 11

cuttlebone, 64

dechlorinated water, 36, 50

Ecuadorian, 16, 17, 65

eggs, 15, 63, 64, 85

exoskeleton, 19

exotic shells online, 36

eye stalks, 21

eyes, 16, 17, 21

fertilizers, 61

Florida Keys, 16

food, 14, 21, 31, 49, 53, 55

fruit, 14, 62, 66

gills, 21, 44, 56

grooming, 21

groups, 13, 24

hairspray, 55

Handfeeding, 68

head, 19, 28, 102

hermies, 2, 12, 14, 15, 16, 17, 22, 25, 28, 30, 33, 35, 37, 40, 41, 42, 43, 44, 45, 47, 48, 49, 51, 52, 102, 103

humidity, 22, 26, 37, 40, 42, 44, 45, 58, 73, 75, 102

Indonesian Purple Hermit Crab, 18

intellectual stimulation, 15, 31

isolation tank, 70, 75, 76, 77

land, 11, 12

legs, 12, 13, 16, 17, 18, 20, 21, 22, 30, 103

maxillipeds, 21

mist, 56, 57, 58, 59, 69, 75, 102

mold, 32, 35, 45, 47, 58, 66, 67, 73

nocturnal, 13, 14, 43, 46, 49

ocean, 13, 30, 35, 50, 85

omnivores, 60, 62

organic fruit, 61

Paguroidea, 11

painting, 55

parasites, 36, 48

pellet food, 66

pesticides, 61

pet trade, 17, 18

pinchers, 12, 16, 20, 63

preservatives, 60, 63

Purple Pincher, 16, 17

Rugs or Ruggies, 18

salt, 49, 50, 51, 53, 63

scavengers, 55

snail shells, 13, 19, 54

soldier crab, 16

species, 2, 15, 16, 17, 18, 19, 24, 29, 31, 46

strawberries, 61

Strawberry Hermit Crab, 18

Index

Strawberry Hermit Crabs, 65

sugar, 63

sun-dried Red Shrimp food, 65

sunlight, 13, 26, 31, 42

tank, 2, 24, 26, 31, 32, 37, 38, 41, 42, 43, 44, 45, 46, 51, 53, 54, 56, 66, 105

tannin, 63

thorax, 19, 21

Uca pugnax, 105

vegetables, 60, 61, 65, 66

veterinarian, 27

West Atlantic crab, 16

Zoo Med, 65

CPSIA information can be obtained at www.ICGtesting.com
Printed in the USA
LVOW12s1728270614

392063LV00013B/746/P